A New Baby
& Other Stories

A New Baby
& Other Stories

By Annita Cole

A NEW BABY
and Other Stories

Published by Annita Cole, Edmonton, Canada

ISBN:

Paperback	978-1-77354-559-2
ebook	978-1-77354-566-0

Publication assistance and digital printing in Canada by

PUBLISHING
PageMaster.ca

Thank You to Anna-Lisa, a dear friend of our family, for editing these stories. Your editing business "Arbordel Editing" has made these stories of my experiences possible.

Thank You also to Valerie MacNall for painting the kitty and the mouse for the story "The IMPORTANCE OF GOD'S FAMILY" Valerie and I attend the same art club. I am not good at drawing hair so asked Valerie to do this one for me. She is a very talented artist and I love her work. She also makes a good friend to have in your life.

Contents

Introduction

My name is Annita Helen Cole, and I am the author of the stories you are about to read. I was born to Don and Helen Cole on a small farm sixteen miles southeast of Rocky Mountain House in Chedderville, Alberta, Canada. For those of you who know where #22 south is, our family lived one mile west of the Dovercourt Hall. Dad and Mom had milk cows, a cow-calf operation, sheep, pigs and horses.

The little girl in the stories is called Neatie. That is me! My family called me Neat or Neatie. I had other nicknames too. The neighbors and my sisters used to call me Pete or Peatie because when I was preschool aged I loved a young man in the district named Pete. When I started working as a cabin leader at Silverside

Gospel camp near Gull Lake, my nickname there became Neatie-Peatie. In later years I had my Sunday school kids call me by that name too.

I was raised with five siblings. We played, fought, worked with and loved each other. We went with the neighbor kids to a country school that had eight grades in one room.

The stories my characters tell are some of the things that happened on or near our little farm.

My hope for the children who read these stories is that they will learn something about how to love others from each one. My inspiration for writing is the explanation of what love is and isn't in 1 Corinthians 13:4-8.

I believe that the love of God and how it is applied to our own hearts and those around us helps us to live a more peaceful life. It is also a command of Jesus to love one another. John 13:34 says, "A new commandment I give unto you, that you love one another; as I have loved you, that you also love one another."

I have not always accomplished this, but it is what I strive for.

I also love to paint, and the pictures you will see in this book are my own. The birds and animals I painted tell the stories, and I hope you enjoy my artwork as well as the stories about my childhood told through their eyes.

–Annita

Annita Cole

A New Baby: The Importance of God's Family

Hi kids! My name is Kenny Kitten! I'm sitting near the wall in a small kitchen in a very small house. I am waiting for a mouse. I'm sure it ran into this very small hole in the wall.

I need to be real quiet if I want to catch that mouse, but I can hear voices behind me and it is so hard to keep still! I live with humans in this very small house. The mice live here too and that's why the humans need me. My little human friend Winnie lives in the house with me. She went away a few weeks ago. I don't know where she is but I sure do miss her!

It is the middle of the night and Mommy and Daddy Human should be sound asleep. But I can hear them walking around and talking instead!

Daddy Human goes outside and soon I hear the tractor start. It makes a terrible noise! The noise is getting fainter. Now I can't hear it at all. Where is Daddy Human going?

Mommy Human sounds like she is having trouble. What is going on? I hear another sound I've never heard before. Let's go see what's happening!

Oh my, it's a very tiny human making all this racket! Mommy Human's brother Max is warming a towel to wrap it in so it doesn't get cold.

Then I hear the tractor coming back! Daddy Human comes in and talks to Mommy, and he looks so pleased with his new baby. They name her Annita! They call her Neatie for short. Maybe she will play with me like Winnie does.

Speaking of Winnie, here she comes back to the house! She went and stayed with Grandma Human for a little while but now she's home safe and sound. Mommy and Daddy Human and Winnie and Annita are all together, snug in their little house.

And of course, I'm still here too! And where oh where is that mouse?

God's Word tells us that God sent His Son, Jesus, to the earth. A young woman called Mary was His earthly Mother and Joseph was her husband. God the Father was and is His heavenly Father. Jesus is the Son of God and the Son of Man.

John tells us in chapter 3 verses 16 and 17 that "God loved the world so much that He gave His only Son so that anyone who believes in Him shall not perish but have eternal life. God did not send His Son into the world to condemn it, but to save it."

This means that we can ask Jesus to forgive our sins and be born into God's family. Jesus told Nicodemus that he needed to be born again. Sin is disobedience to God. That is why we need to repent of our sin and read God's word to see how He wants us to live.

Just like Daddy and Mommy Human were so pleased to have their little family all together, God the Father is so happy when one of His children asks forgiveness and comes home to His loving arms.

Cooper

Annita Cole

A Berry Buzzy Time: Trust

Hi kids! I'm Harry Hawk. I love flying high in the sky and keeping my eye on what happens on the ground. Earth looks so good from up here! There are pastures, sand hills, and trees for me to watch.

I don't see any food yet, but I do see Mommy Human and her little ones coming up the path. They have shiny pails that are clattering and wobbling as they hurry up a winding little trail stretched across the pasture to the sand hills.

Those little ones are chattering loudly to each other. I think every animal along the way will hear them long before they get to the berry patch on the ridge!

They might even be making noise on purpose, so they don't surprise any bears who also like picking berries in the berry patch! I did see a black bear there a few days ago.

I'm looking down on the humans from above now as I move closer to see what they are doing. The little boy human they call Chuck is putting some leaves in his pail so it will fill faster and he can go run and play. Naughty boy!

There is also a little girl called Donna, and she is holding onto the thing around her neck that rings when it moves, so that Mommy Human won't hear it and know where she is. I think they call it a bell?

Now they are all kneeling down in front of the berry bushes on the soft moss. I think those little ones are eating more berries than they are putting in their pails! They are picking for a bit and then playing for a bit. They look pretty happy.

Annita Cole

One of the little girls who they call Neatie has her pail almost full. She is picking faster than the rest. A funny look comes over her face and she stops picking to listen. What does she hear? Is something wrong?

She calls out to Mommy and Mommy answers her. She comes over to where Neatie is kneeling. I think she hears something too! What could it be?

Then Mommy puts a piece of bark under little Neatie's knee. The rest keep picking. When they are finished picking berries from that patch all the children except Neatie go down the path toward their house in the distance. I can hear an angry buzzing sound. What could it be? Why did they leave Neatie behind?

Mommy calls Neatie, and finally she gets up and runs very fast toward Mommy and the other children. Oh! Now I see! There were bees in the ground where Neatie was kneeling. Mommy told her to stay still while she got the other children away and made a plan for Neatie to follow quickly at the right moment.

I can hear and see the bees now! They are coming out of the ground and they are not happy. The humans run away and the bees go about their business. Thank goodness no one got hurt!

In a little while the humans get back to their house and go inside and out of sight. I don't go any closer, because I know this house well. The humans have a long wooden stick that makes a big bang, and they point it at you if you get too close to their chickens.

I will see the human family the next time they leave their yard! Until then I will think about the trust little Neatie had in her mother. She was scared and wanted to run, but she did what Mama told her to do, and her obedience kept her and everyone else safe.

God wants us to trust Him, for the simple reason that He can be trusted! The book of

Annita Cole

Proverbs is found in the Old Testament. In chapter 3 verses 3-5 it says, "Trust in the Lord with all your heart; do not depend on your own understanding. Seek his will in all you do, and he will show you which path to take."

Just like Neatie trusted her mother and stayed still until she was told to move even though she wanted to run away, we need to trust God even when it doesn't make sense to us. He is a good Father who wants the best for His children.

Annita Cole

Cricket Has a Story to Tell

Hi kids! My name is Cricket, and I'm a horse! This other horse is Goldie.The human family who lives on the farm uses us to haul logs and hay, and they even ride us sometimes.

I hear the old wooden door on the farmhouse bang shut as my three little humans Winnie, Neatie, and Beryl run down the path to the gate where my friend Goldie and I are hooked up to the big, old hayrack.

We like Winnie, Neatie and Beryl. They are good to us, and we try not to kick them or step on them! The girls climb up on the hayrack and then Daddy Human flicks the reins and clicks his tongue. This is our signal to start pulling the hayrack forward, so we do!

The old wooden rack started to move slowly with its familiar creaks and groans. We passed the house, turned onto the road, and started for the far field. We are going to get a load of hay for the animals in the barnyard. That hay sure tastes good to Goldie and I at the end of a long day's work.

It is a sunny spring day. The water is running, the birds are singing, and it feels good to be alive. I think the coyote that runs out of the brush and across the road in front of us agrees with me! He disappears into the brush on the other side.

This upsets a squirrel who starts up an endless chatter of "watch out watch out watch out!" The two dogs stay behind to bark at the squirrel while we plod on. The girls are still giggling and talking about the coyote when we pull into the field and up to the haystack.

Daddy Human had a lot of work to do that day. While he hitches his lines and starts forking hay, the girls jump down to play and hunt for mice. They come to a small muddy pond. It looks inviting even to me, and little Beryl is quite interested in going in.

Winnie and Neatie try to stop her but she walks into the muddy water anyway. Soon her little feet are stuck in the oozing, sucking mud. She works and cries and cries and works but she can't get her feet loose!

Winnie runs for help and Neatie stays with Beryl. Beryl begs and pleads with Neatie to try and get her out before Daddy Human sees what has happened. Neatie is upset and frightened but she goes in after Beryl anyway.

Splash, squish, suck, and Neatie is just as stuck as Beryl! Now there are two frightened little humans up to their knees in the mud. Winnie comes running with help and Daddy Human pulls them out of the mud. He is very angry with my little friends and yells angry words at them while he works to get them free.

Then it is time to go home, and the girls climb up onto the hayrack and sit with their muddy feet hanging over it. They felt so bad about what they had done, I can tell. Daddy Human was so angry. I pulled them all the way home and I thought about why that was so.

I decided he was angry because the girls had wasted his time. They didn't mean to, but when they got stuck Daddy Human had to stop working and pull them out. That must be why he was so upset.

That night when I was eating my hay I got to thinking about how anger hurts everyone. It hurt the little girls who did not mean to upset their daddy. It even hurt Daddy Human because being angry is not comfortable or nice.

I don't know everything about humans but I know that anger is not good. You need to think before you say anything when someone makes you angry. You can really hurt people when you yell at them. Could it be that Daddy Human got

Annita Cole

sucked into angry feelings, just like the girls got sucked into the mud?

Proverbs 15:18 tells us that "a hot-tempered person stirs up conflict, but the one who is patient calms a quarrel." That just means that when you lash out in anger, you can start a fight or hurt someone's feelings. Psalms 103:8 tells us that "The Lord is...slow to anger, abounding in love." God does not get angry quickly. Humans who want to follow what the Bible says need to ask God to help them respond to others with love, even when they are angry.

I hope that the next time his girls do something silly that makes him upset, Daddy Human will remember that yelling in anger doesn't help anyone! God wants us to be slow to anger instead.

Annita Cole

Envy and the Trouble it Brings

Hi kids! I'm Ned Nuthatch. I'm sitting in an old tree watching Daddy Human and some of his little ones. I think they are going to make rope today! On Daddy Human's farm he makes a lot of things that other people just buy, and rope is one of them.

I can see them setting up a simple machine with three wheels and three hooks. It's the rope maker! They are taking three strands of baler twine and looping it over the hooks. Oh, I see! Now they will use the machine to twist the twine strings together to make one strand. Isn't that clever?

Oh my! They have stopped making rope because one little girl is crying. They call her

Marilyn when I see them playing together near my tree. Oh dear, her hair is all twisted in with the rope! One of the others runs away and comes back with a knife. Daddy Human has to cut her hair off to get her free.

How could that have happened? The little girl they call Donna is smiling behind Daddy's back. I bet she had something to do with it! She's always been envious of Marilyn's beautiful, blonde, silky hair. Do you know what envy is? Envy means wishing something belongs to you instead of your friend. Donna's hair is white, fine and hard to work with, and she wishes her hair was more like Marilyn's. Yes, I bet Donna's the culprit alright.

They finish the rope and little Marilyn isn't smiling! She is very sad about her hair. Donna's envy made her do something very unkind.

God doesn't like envy. God's Word says in 1 Corinthians 13:4 that "Love is patient, love is kind. It does not envy..." This means that if you love someone like God loves us, you don't envy them. It's not easy to obey God all the time, but if we say we are sorry He will forgive us.

I would like to hear Donna say she is sorry, but I don't think it will happen right away. Fortunately, God is patient and Donna really does love her friend. I'm going to go back to finding more bugs and hope she comes around soon!

Annita Cole

Fearfully and Wonderfully Made

Hi kids, my name is Sarah Swallow! I'm sitting in the loft of the big Cole barn. I'm watching and listening to two little humans who live on the farm. Their names are Neatie and Marilyn.

I see them a lot as they always come here to talk when they don't want anyone else to hear them. When you live in a family of six kids, you always have someone listening in! If you can sneak to the barn and crawl into the loft without being seen, you can tell your best friend what you really think about things.

Neatie does not look happy. I'm sorry about that because she likes to talk and laugh and I enjoy listening to her! I'll keep watching and listening and maybe I will be able to figure out what is making her angry today.

I have lots of time to listen since I'm sitting on my eggs and waiting for them to hatch! Neatie is talking now. She is telling her friend all the reasons she is unhappy.

She says she doesn't understand why her sisters Winnie and Beryl got such nice hair and she didn't. She thinks they are very pretty and she is just plain. They have lovely singing voices and good musical ears while she sings off key and has a soft plain voice.

Then, to make things worse, Neatie heard the grownups talking about how wonderful her sisters are, and how she is the most mischievous child they have ever seen.

Neatie tells Marilyn she has been reading in her Bible to see if she can figure out if God thinks she is plain and not as good as her sisters too. She wants to know if God loves her or if he just didn't care how he made her.

I am sad for little Neatie. No wonder she isn't happy! I want to know the answer as well so I will keep listening. Then I hear Marilyn tell Neatie that God says we are fearfully and wonderfully made. She said we can read this in Psalms 139 verse 18. She asked Neatie if she believes God's Word is true?

Neatie says she does believe God's Word is true. Marilyn tells her she should ask God to forgive her for thinking He didn't care about how He made her just because she isn't the same as everyone else. I see Neatie bow her head and ask Jesus to forgive her. She looks happy again, thank goodness!

I'm only a bird, but God made me too. Maybe I'm not the prettiest bird God ever made but he made me for a reason and that's all that matters. When I flit and fly around the barnyard eating all the bugs I can find, I help everyone on this farm and that makes me so happy.

And when the sun hits my feathers just right, I shine so beautifully. It's all about your perspective really!

What about you, reading this story? What do you think about yourself?

Jesus says you are beautifully and wonderfully made. He always tells the Truth, so we can believe Him! God cannot lie for He is Spirit and Truth. John 14:6 says "I am the Way, the Truth, and the Life." God made you the way you are for a reason, and you can trust Him to know what He is doing and have your very best in mind.

I hope the next time Neatie and Marilyn come to the barn to chat, it's about something they are thankful for. I do love hearing their happy little voices chattering away as I sit on my nest!

Annita Cole ©

Annita Cole

The Snatched Ball Glove: Being Kind to Others

Hi kids, I'm Billy Blue Bird! I have a nest in a tree across the road from a school. I like to go over to the school when the kids are outside and watch them play. Today they are playing a game of baseball on the ball diamond.

Everyone was having fun until a little boy named Chuck ripped his sister Neatie's ball glove out of her hand and ran away with it! He thought it was a good joke, but Neatie did not. She ran after him while he tried to dodge her, this way and that!

Chuck jumped the school fence into a farmer's field, and Neatie jumped the fence after him. Chuck jumped back and Neatie did the same. But this time, she did not see the top wire! It was slack and hanging down, and she caught her foot in it as she jumped. Down she went, and laid there on the ground with her left elbow sticking out at an odd angle.Oh dear!

The kids gathered around and little Doris told Neatie not to move. Clayton gave up his glove to put under Neatie's head. Neatie's brother Chuck was sorry she got hurt. Geraldyn was crying and everyone was sad for Neatie.The teacher sent someone to Neatie's farm to get her Dad. He came, and they all helped Neatie up and into the truck. I heard one of the kids say they were headed for the hospital.

I saw it all and I am very impressed with how the kids were so kind and concerned. It is so good when humans are kind to those around them. We all need to treat others the way we want to be treated. Neatie was very blessed to have such kind friends in her time of trouble.

Annita Cole

I'm sure her arm will get fixed up and she will be back at school with her friends in no time!

I want you to think about how you treat the other kids around you. Are you kind? Can you be counted on? I sure hope so. Galatians 5:22 says that the Holy Spirit produces kindness in our lives. When we are kind to others, we are showing them God's love.

After seeing Neatie's friends take care of her, I'm going to try being more kind to the crow who lives next door to me. I think my life would be easier and better if we were friends.

Cooper

Annita Cole

A Potato Picker Gets Caught: The Sin of Stealing

Hi kids, It's Harry Hawk again, remember me? I told you the story about the berry pickers and the bees! I'm much closer to the farm buildings today because the humans I told you about before are digging potatoes.

Daddy Human has a horse and plow, and he is using them to dig the potatoes out of the ground. The small humans are picking the potatoes up off the ground and taking them into the house and down to the cellar. This is an important job, since those potatoes will help feed the humans during the long winter!

I can see the small humans taking turns. First little Winnie takes potatoes, and then Neatie, and then someone else, and so on. There are quite a few of them. When there is a big job to do, it's good to have a lot of hands to share the work.

This job is taking all afternoon! I have noticed that there's something different about Neatie's turn. She is inside the house longer than her sisters are when they carry potatoes to the cellar. I wonder why?

Daddy Human is finally done digging! I watch him put the horse away and go up to the house. I think I hear someone crying now, who could that be?

I hear the small humans say that Daddy Human is getting Neatie in trouble. For what, I wonder? I listen very carefully, and I hear them say that Neatie was stealing raisins from the kitchen when she took her potatoes into the house. That's why it was taking her so much longer to come back outside!

She thought it was alright because the raisins belonged to the whole family. But Mommy Human told her that if she ate most of the raisins herself, then no one else would get their share. She explained that raisins are to put inside cookies so everyone in the family can have a fair share.

Neatie didn't understand it until she was caught, but when she took the raisins for herself, she was stealing them. Exodus 20:15 says we are not to steal. Stealing is wrong because when you take something that doesn't belong to you, you are keeping others from using it too.

This got me thinking. I steal little chicks from the chicken coop if the small humans don't have the long stick that shoots fire outside with them to chase me away. I'm starting to wonder if I should stay out in the field where the mice are.

I can still see a lot from there, and it's much safer. I don't think I'll steal my little brother's mice anymore either.

What about you? Have you ever taken anything that is not yours? If you want to love others like Jesus loves you then you will have to stop. If I can do it and Neatie can do it, so can you! Jesus will forgive you if you ask Him. He loves you.

Annita Cole

The Little Girl Who Lied

Hi kids! I'm Benny Blue Jay and I'm on this limb trying to get a better look at Daddy Human and his kids. Everyone looks sad, and I wonder if it's because I heard Daddy Human say he took Mommy Human to the bus station. He said she would get on a train in a place called Rocky Mountain House and then take a train to Enderby, British Columbia, wherever that is.

Even though they are sad, Daddy and the little humans are going to get water from the well and take it to the sheep, because the sheep are thirsty. Little Neatie is crying and I think Daddy is nervous about having the kids to look after all by himself, and that must be why he started yelling at Neatie for crying.

Then he asks Neatie what the problem is in a harsh voice. She doesn't want to tell him that she is crying because Mommy isn't at home and she is worried and scared. What will they all do until Mom gets back? So instead, she points at her little brother Chuck and says he hit her, even though he didn't. Then Daddy is mad at little Chuck, and spanks him.

I can see that Neatie is feeling sad and guilty for getting Chuck in trouble with her big lie.

But lying didn't make anything better. Neatie felt even worse after she lied, but she was afraid to own up to what she had done. Poor little Chuck was crying now, and he didn't tell anyone that he hadn't hit Neatie.

They went to the pump house and filled up some five gallon pails with water and put them on a toboggan so they wouldn't have to carry them. When they were ready to pour the water into the trough, a pig came along and pushed the pails of water over! They had to go back to the well and get more water. Daddy was not happy and the little humans were still sad. Nothing is going right today!

Lies are terrible things. They are a sin against God and against the person you tell the lie about. John 4:24 says, "God is spirit, and those who worship Him must worship in spirit and truth." God doesn't lie at all. Satan is the one who starts lies. He is God's enemy and ours too, if we want to follow Jesus. So if you are tempted to lie to get out of trouble, just remember that you are in more trouble when you lie than when you tell the truth.

And, don't forget that you can ask Jesus to forgive you. He will! 1 John 1:9 tells us that "If we confess our sins, he is faithful and just to forgive us our sins." We can believe this because it's in the Bible. God never lies, remember?

Daddy and the littles got the chores done and went into their house. I hope Neatie confessed to what she had done and made things right with Chuck and Daddy Human. I have to get back to finding food, and I'll need to tell my mommy the truth about where I have been and why I am late for supper! Goodbye for now!

Annita Cole

Annita Cole

The Peace That Comes from God

Hi kids! I'm Sam the sandhill crane. I see some little humans playing in the dugout and riding a raft. They are laughing and having a wonderful time! They have little tin cans that they are dipping in the water. What are they doing?

Oh I see what they are doing! They are scooping up tadpoles to look at and play with. Do you know what a tadpole is? It's a baby frog. I eat tadpoles and frogs, so I hope they put the tadpoles back in the water when they are done playing.

After a bit I hear Mommy Human calling the little ones. They bring their raft up on the banks of the pond and start walking toward the barnyard.

Then, I see a killdeer running in front of them, and it looks like it has a broken wing. The human kids see it too and try to catch it. When the humans get close the killdeer flies away. It was only pretending to have a broken wing to lead the humans away from its nest. How clever!

As they walk, they see a horse with a new foal and stop to have a look. Then they decide to lick salt from the block on the ground near the horse. They also stop to have a drink of water from the well. Finally, they arrive at the house where Mommy Human is.

I get to thinking that these little humans must really love each other. They are always together, joking and sharing adventures. Watching them is very peaceful. God's love for us and humans' love for each other is really special.

Annita Cole

Romans 5:1 says, "Therefore, since we have been justified by faith, we have peace with God through our Lord Jesus Christ." This tells us that we have peace with God because of what Jesus has done for us on the Cross.

God loves us, so that we can love Him and those around us.This is where our peace comes from. I hope you find the peace these kids have. Now it's time for me to wander off to the pond to eat those tadpoles! I'll talk to you again sometime.

Cooper

Annita
Cole ©

Annita Cole

Respect for Others

Hi kids! It's me again, Harry Hawk! I can hear my old friend Neatie's voice so I fly over the human house and follow her and Winnie. It's always interesting keeping an eye on these little humans!

I see Winnie has a note from Mommy Human. If they didn't have a note then their Aunt would discipline them and send them home. The note says Mommy Human needs a break, so she is sending them to their Aunt Jaunita and their cousins Viola and Arla for a few hours.

They get across the road safely and through the trees to their Aunty's house. Their auntie's dog Bruno likes them, and barks a welcome as they arrive. Bunnie and Jill, the lambs, romp up and say "baa baa baa". They say hi like this whenever the human kids visit.

They go into the house and Aunty is happy to see them. I watch through the window since no one invites me in! They play with Aunty's toys for a while and then spot a special doll that belongs to Arla. They ask Aunty if they can play with it but Aunty says no as Arla isn't there to make sure it doesn't get broken. Neatie wants to argue with Aunty about the doll as it looks like it would be fun to play with.

But she doesn't argue, because she remembers just in time that she shouldn't demand her own way. God's Word says this in I Corinthians 13:5: "Love does not dishonor others, it is not self-seeking, it is not easily angered." Annita shows love to her Aunty by respecting her wishes.

The little humans play with the lambs for a bit longer and then start for home. On the way, I think about how Neatie is learning a lot from her parents and family about what it is like to love others and not always put yourself first. I'm really proud of her! I think I'll go home now and hope to talk to you again.

Annita Cole

Learning to Knit: A Lesson in Patience

Hi kids! My name is Charlie Chickadee and right now I am sitting on a broken tree. I can see into the window of the old house on this farm and I'm watching the humans inside. Daddy Human is playing a game with some of the little humans. Mommy Human is knitting a pair of mittens, and one of the little humans is knitting her own little mitten too.

Her name is Neatie, and she is having trouble because this is her first knitting lesson and it is not easy! She lets some of the stitches slip off the needle and gets very frustrated. She is so upset that she throws the unfinished mitten across the room!

Mommy looks up from her knitting and says, "It doesn't matter how many times you throw it Neatie, you will still have to finish knitting that mitten if you want your hands to be warm for school this fall." So Neatie goes and picks the mitten up, puts the stitches back on the needle, and keeps on knitting.

This is not the first time I have seen Mommy being patient with her little humans. She is a very good teacher. I have seen her teaching them to give the orphan lambs their bottle, pack water for the chickens, sweep the steps, cook simple meals, and help with their younger siblings.

Neatie is going to have to learn to be patient just like Mommy Human if she is going to finish her mittens for school! God is patient, and He wants us to learn to be like him. 1 Corinthians 13:4 says, "Love is patient and kind." God is love, which means he is even more patient with us than Mommy Human is with her little humans!

I hope Neatie will be patient enough to get her mittens finished before she needs them to keep her hands warm on her walk to and from school. Thinking about patience makes me wonder if I should learn to be patient with the dog that guards this place. He chases me and I don't like it. Maybe he could be patient with me too! I will say good-bye for now, and I hope I get to talk to you again.

Thank you for completing this book.

We would love if you could help by posting a review at your book retailer and on the PageMaster Publishing site. It only takes a minute and it would really help others by giving them an idea of your experience.

Thanks

Annita Cole at the PageMaster Store
https://pagemasterpublishing.ca/by/annita-cole/

To order more copies of this book, find books by other Canadian authors, or make inquiries about publishing your own book, contact PageMaster at:

PageMaster Publication Services Inc.
11340-120 Street, Edmonton, AB T5G 0W5
books@pagemaster.ca
780-425-9303

catalogue and e-commerce store
PageMasterPublishing.ca/Shop